# TABLE GRACES *for the* FAMILY

# TABLE GRACES *for the* FAMILY

*A Special Collection of Blessings and Prayers*

W PUBLISHING GROUP
A Division of Thomas Nelson Publishers
*Since 1798*
www.wpublishinggroup.com

W Publishing books may be purchased in bulk for educational, business, fund-raising, or sales promotional use. For information, please e-mail SpecialMarkets@ThomasNelson.com.

Published by W Publishing Group, a division of Thomas Nelson, Inc., P.O. Box 141000, Nashville, Tennessee 37214.



Selections for this edition of *Table Graces for the Family* were made by Laura Kendall.

**Library of Congress Cataloging-in-Publication Data**

Table graces for the family : a special collection of blessings and prayers.
p. cm.
ISBN 0-8499-1845-6
1. Grace at meals—Christianity. 2. Family—Prayer-books and devotions—English. I. W Publishing Group.
BV283.G7T28 2005
242'.8—dc22

2004029447

*Printed in the United States of America*

05 06 07 08 QWM 6 5 4 3 2 1

# Contents

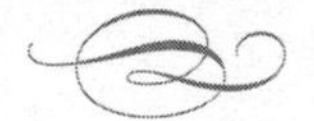

*Introduction* . . . . . . . . . . . . . . . . . . . . . . . . . . *vii*

1 Morning Graces . . . . . . . . . . . . . . . . . . . . . . . . . 1

2 Children's Graces . . . . . . . . . . . . . . . . . . . . . . . 11

3 Graces for Every Day . . . . . . . . . . . . . . . . . . . . . 23

4 Graces from the Bible . . . . . . . . . . . . . . . . . . . . 61

5 Poetic Graces . . . . . . . . . . . . . . . . . . . . . . . . . 71

6 Graces from Other Cultures . . . . . . . . . . . . . . . 81

7 Musical Graces . . . . . . . . . . . . . . . . . . . . . . . . 93

8 Graces for Holidays and Holy Days . . . . . . 101

9 Graces for Special Occasions . . . . . . . . . . . . 133

10 Evening Graces . . . . . . . . . . . . . . . . . . . . . . . 153

11 Our Family's Own Special Graces . . . . . . . . . 157

*Acknowledgments* . . . . . . . . . . . . . . . . . . . . . . 161

# Introduction

*"God is great, and God is good,*
*And we thank Him for our food."*

These words perhaps form the first prayer you remember praying. If so, you're like countless others who began to learn the great lesson of gratitude—at mealtime. And you've never forgotten that lesson.

The dinner table—or breakfast table—is often the only place where families pause and give thanks to God for His blessings. For those who remember to do it, saying grace serves not only as a time to thank God for food, but to recognize that He is with us, not only during this meal, but throughout our lives. Though we call it "saying grace," it is really a time when we acknowledge *His* grace in our lives.

Our table blessings, though, sometimes become monotonous. We recite memorized prayers from our childhood or repeat short prayers we've used for years, and we sometimes might wonder if even God is bored hearing the same old things. *Of course, He isn't.* God loves hearing our prayers, no matter how simple or repetitive they may be. But our mealtime graces can become richer and more meaningful for every family member, and this little book was compiled to help you do that.

We have included graces and prayers for all times of the day, for special days, for ordinary days, for holidays, and more. When you're too sleepy to think of the words to pray at breakfast, turn to the "Morning Graces" section and read one of the selections that offers thanks for the night's rest and a new day. When your children are old enough to read, let them choose one of the simple prayers from the "Children's Graces" section, where they will enjoy learning the traditional blessings as well as the lighter ones that can be sung to familiar tunes.

The longest section is called "Graces for Every Day," because that's where most of our lives are lived—in the everyday. Here the graces range from simple prayers of two or three sentences to longer poetic prayers. These prayers offer thanks for "an amazing variety of foods to eat: fruits and vegetables, breads and grains, meat and fish, milk and eggs, and sweet desserts" . . . "for taste buds that relish the food placed before us" . . . and even "for the one who invented the refrigerator to keep our food from spoiling."

For times when we want to draw on the talent of poets and saints who lived long ago, we have included "Poetic Graces." The beloved prayer of St. Francis of Assisi—"Lord, make me an instrument of Your peace"—is included, as well as prayer-poems from Robert Burns, Robert Louis Stevenson, and E. E. Cummings.

"Graces from Other Cultures" includes graces from Africa, Brazil, Hawaii, and Argentina, to name a few, and offers an opportunity to teach your children about a wider world. Families often enjoy singing their blessings, and you can expand your repertoire by using songs from the "Musical Graces" section.

Holidays bring their own special needs and opportunities to be thankful. In "Graces for Holidays and Holy Days" you'll find prayers for every season—from New Year's Day to the Fourth of July and through Christmas. There are even prayers to use when you're on vacation. Your family may also want to use the prayers for the special days of the church year, including graces for Ash Wednesday, Good Friday, Easter, Advent, and other holy days.

Are you celebrating a birthday, an anniversary, Mother's Day, Father's Day, a family reunion, the first day of school, or a new home? A refreshing collection of prayers is included to help you find words of gratitude for all these blessings.

We hope these table graces will be an inspiration for your family to stay in the habit of thanking God daily for every gift He provides. We encourage you to use them often, either as written or as a springboard for saying thanks in your own words. As your children listen to you pray from your heart, they also will learn to pray and grow in their gratitude for all of God's gifts.

We pray that this book will be a blessing to both you and your family—and that each prayer you pray will increase your appreciation for God's goodness as He provides for all your needs.

—Laura Kendall

## The Lord's Prayer

Our Father which art in heaven,
Hallowed be thy name.
Thy kingdom come.
Thy will be done
in earth, as it is in heaven.
Give us this day our daily bread.
And forgive us our debts,
as we forgive our debtors.
And lead us not into temptation,
but deliver us from evil:
For thine is the kingdom, and the power, and
the glory, forever. Amen.

—Matthew 6:9–13 (KJV)

# I

# *Morning Graces*

For all Thy Blessings,
For this new morning and its light,
The rest and shelter of the night,
For health and food, love and friends,
For every gift His goodness sends,
We thank Thee, gracious Lord.
Amen.

—ANONYMOUS

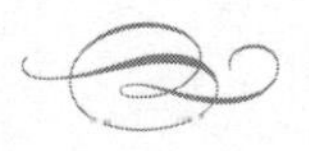

For the night's rest, the morning meal, the new day, and all the blessings it may bring, we give You grateful thanks, our Father. Help us to serve You by serving others; through Jesus Christ our Lord. Amen.

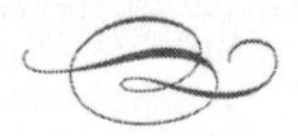

We thank You, Father, for this new day which You are giving us, and for all it brings to remind us of Your love. May this food strengthen us for our duties, and may our lives today be for Your glory and honor. Amen.

Lord,

Our hearts worship You this morning. You have kept us in safety throughout the night, and we are thankful for Your protecting care. We thank You for this food, and may the strength we receive from it be spent in Your service. We pray through Jesus. Amen.

Thank You, God, that we don't have to worry about the sun rising every morning, just as we don't need to worry about Your providing for our needs, as long as we trust You. We are eternally grateful for Your constant love and care. We humbly ask that You bless this food and restore our bodies with it. Amen.

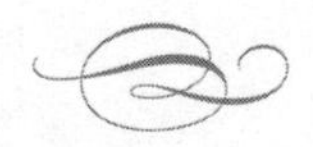

God of new beginnings,

You touch me
and I wake
to find a
brand new day.

The day is ripe
with all the possibility
it can hold.

Yesterday is forgotten
and all that matters
is today.

What will I do?
Show me, O Lord.
How will I live?
Guide me, O God.

May I be as good
to others today
as You are always
to me.
Amen.

We give You thanks, O heavenly Father, who has kept us through the night. We pray that You will guide us this day to serve You better. May we always praise Your name. Through Jesus Christ our Lord. Amen.

Lord,

Each morning new mercies dawn. Teach us how to begin and end each day with praise and prayer. May the food that has been prepared for us make us mindful of Your constant love and sustaining grace. Amen.

Grant us, Lord, to live this day in gladness and peace. We pray that we will overcome the temptations of the day and truly live for You. We praise You for Your guidance in our lives and pray that we will continually strive to be more like Christ. We pray through His name. Amen.

Give us this day
our daily bread, O Father
in heaven, and grant that we
who are filled with good things
from Your open hand
may never close our hearts
to the hungry, the homeless,
and the poor;
in the name of the Father,
and of the Son,
and of the Holy Spirit.

—ABBEY OF NEW CLAIRVAUX, VINA, CALIFORNIA

For flowers that bloom about our feet,
 Father, we thank Thee;
For tender grass so fresh and sweet,
 Father, we thank Thee;
For song of bird and hum of bee,
For all things fair we hear or see,
 Father in heaven, we thank Thee.

For this new morning with its light,
 Father, we thank Thee;
For rest and shelter of the night,
 Father, we thank Thee;
For health and food, for love and friends,
For everything Thy goodness sends,
 Father in heaven, we thank Thee.

—RALPH WALDO EMERSON (1803–1882)

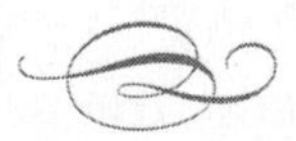

Most holy and ever-loving God, we thank You once more for the quiet rest of the night that has gone by, for the new promise that has come with this fresh morning, and for the hope of this day. While we have slept, the world in which we live has swept on, and we have rested under the shadow of Your love. May we trust You this day for all the needs of the body, the soul, and the spirit. Give us this day our daily bread. Amen.

—Robert Collyer

Lord, we thank You for the gift of sleep, for our health and strength, for the beginning of another day, and for our daily food. We pray that we will use the new opportunities for work and service to their fullest. Help us to keep our trust and faith in You. We praise You for the gift of Your Son. It is in His name that we pray. Amen.

ather,

You have mercifully kept us through the night. How wonderful is Your continued goodness. Protect us this day. Guide and assist us in all our thoughts, words, and actions. Make us willing to do what You wish. In the matchless name of Jesus we pray. Amen.

# 2

# *Children's Graces*

Thank You for the world so sweet,
Thank You for the food we eat,
Thank You for the birds that sing,
Thank You, God, for everything.
Amen.

—Edith Rutter Leatham

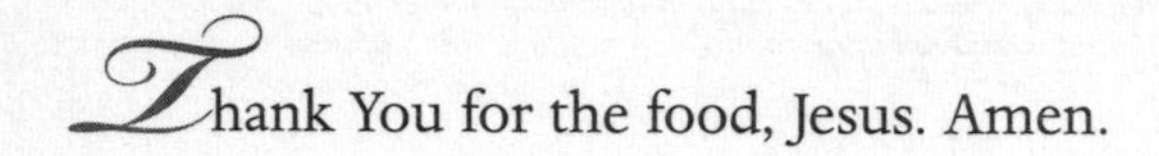

Thank You for the food, Jesus. Amen.

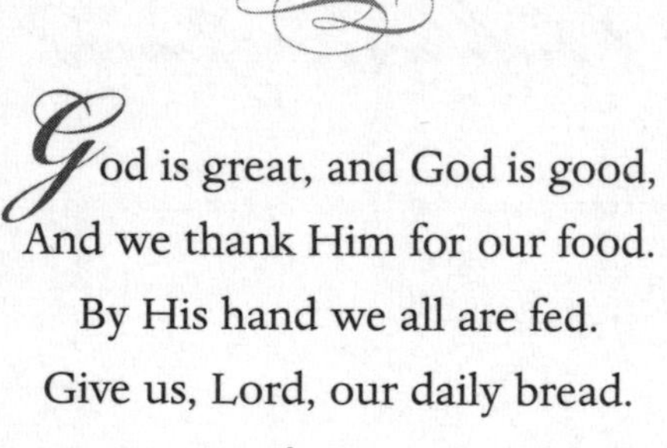

God is great, and God is good,
And we thank Him for our food.
By His hand we all are fed.
Give us, Lord, our daily bread.
Amen.

—AUTHOR UNKNOWN

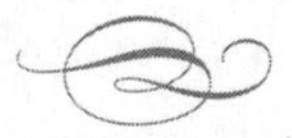

Thank You, God, for food so good.
Lord, help us do the things we should.
Amen.

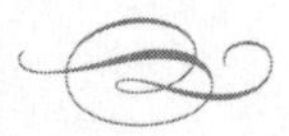

We thank You, loving Father,
For all Your tender care,
For food and clothes and shelter,
And all Your world so fair.
Amen.

For health and strength and daily food,
we give Thee thanks, O Lord.
Amen.

Dear God,

Thank You for the winter's snow,

Thank You for this time to grow.

Thank You for spring flowers bright,

Thank You for my bed at night.

Thank You, Lord, for summer's heat,

Thank You for this food to eat.

Amen.

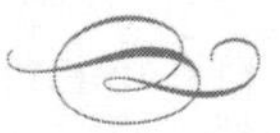

Lord, teach us to love as only You can.

Thank You for giving us so much in life to love.

Thank You for this food You've given us,

and thank You for Jesus.

Amen.

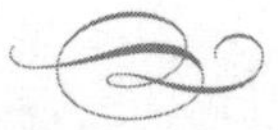

O God, please be with me through this day. Fill my heart with love for You and everyone I meet. If someone is sad, help me to comfort that person. If someone is unfair, help me to forgive. If someone is angry, help me to be patient. If someone especially needs love, help me to be loving. And when things go wrong today, let me remember to ask Your help. In Jesus' name. Amen.

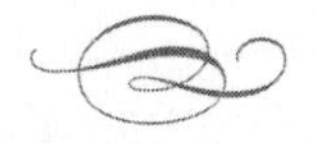

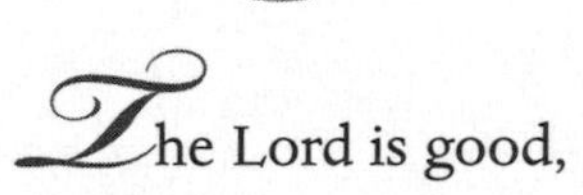

The Lord is good,<br>
He gives us food,<br>
To help us grow up strong.<br>
And as we grow,<br>
His love we'll show,<br>
And praise Him all day long.<br>
Amen.

Dear Lord,

Thank You for giving me another day. Help me to concentrate on my work at school, to be respectful to my teachers, to be fair when I play games, to be obedient to my parents, to be a willing helper at home, and to be kind to my friends. Help me to make this day more pleasant for everyone by being cheerful. Please bless my family and all those I love. In Jesus' name. Amen.

Dear God,

Thank You for this food,

and thank You for my friends.

Teach me to share with everyone,

even when it's hard to.

Amen.

We thank Thee, Lord, for happy hearts,

For rain and sunny weather.

We thank Thee, Lord, for this our food,

And that we are together.

—EMILIE FENDALL JOHNSON

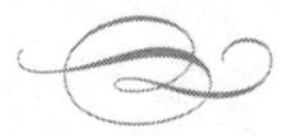

O God, bless all the people that I love at home, in school, and far away. Guide them by day and by night and keep them always under Your loving care. And, Lord, bless also the people I don't love the way I should. Teach me to love them and understand them in spite of our differences. Help me to forgive those who act badly toward me and especially bless them because they need Your love as well as mine. In Jesus' name. Amen.

Thank You, Lord, for food and drink,
For warm and sunny weather,
Thank You, Lord, for all we have,
And that we're all together.
Thank You, Lord, for Jesus Christ,
Thanks for our salvation.
Thanks for dying on the cross,
For us and every nation. Amen.

—GIRL SCOUT CAMPFIRE GRACE
(TUNE: "YANKEE DOODLE")

Thank, thank, thank You, God,
Thank You now we pray.
You have given all we need
To live through every day.

—GIRL SCOUT CAMPFIRE GRACE
(TUNE: "ROW, ROW, ROW YOUR BOAT")

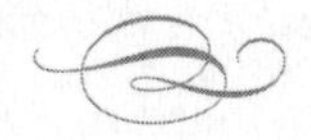

## JOHNNY APPLESEED GRACE

Oh, the Lord's been good to me.
And so I thank the Lord
For giving me the things I need:
The sun, the rain, and the appleseed;
Oh, the Lord's been good to me.
I wake up every day
As happy as can be,
Because I know the Lord is there
Watchin' over all my friends and me
The Lord is good to me.

## Group Prayer

Oh, the Lord is good to us
And so we thank the Lord
For giving us the best of friends
The kind of love that never ends
The Lord is good to us.

Thank you, Lord, for blessings sweet,
Thank you, Lord, for food to eat.
Amen.

## For Summer Vacation

Thank You, God, that school is out and we have the whole summer to play and have fun. Thank You for mornings to sleep late, for sunny, warm days, for swimming pools, for baseball, for hot dogs and ice cream. And now, we thank You for this food. In Jesus' name. Amen.

Gracias, arigato, merci beaucoup,
*(clap clap)*
Gracias, arigato, merci beaucoup,
*(clap clap)*
I can say thank You to God
*(clap clap)*
in Spanish, Japanese, French words, too.
*(clap clap)*

—Children's rhyme

# 3
# Graces for Every Day

Lord, bless our meal,
and as You satisfy
the needs of each
of us, make us
mindful of the
needs of others.

—Mount of St. Mary's Abbey,
Wrentham, Massachusetts

Bless these Thy gifts, most gracious God
From whom all goodness springs;
Make clean our hearts and feed our souls
With good and joyful things.

—TRADITIONAL CHRISTIAN GRACE

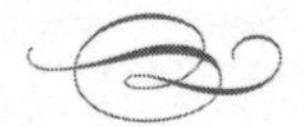

Before You, God, we bow
To pray this to You now,
Lord, thank You for this food,
And help us to be good.
Amen.

Heavenly Father, You give us our daily bread and so much more. Thank You for our family, for the joy that each person at this table brings to our lives; for our home, which is warm and safe; for our friends, who enrich our lives; and most of all, for Your love, which sustains us every day. In Jesus' name. Amen.

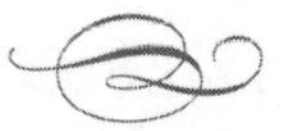

Our loving heavenly Father, as we sit around this table, our hearts unite in praising You for the blessings of this day. Amen.

Come, Lord Jesus, be our guest;
And let these gifts to us be blessed. Amen.

*To be said while holding hands:*

May the love that is in my heart
pass from my hand to yours.

—TRADITIONAL AMERICAN GRACE

Father, we are so thankful for times like this, to enjoy good food and be with those we love. We thank You for opportunities to get to know one another better. Help us always to find the time in our lives for those we love. Now, bless this meal and all we say as our bonds of love grow deeper. In the name of Christ, who taught us to love as You have loved us. Amen.

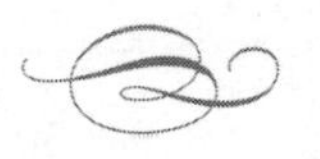

God to enfold me, God to surround me,
God in my speaking, God in my thinking.
God in my sleeping, God in my waking,
God in my watching, God in my hoping.
God in my life, God in my lips,
God in my soul, God in my heart.
God in my sufficing, God in my slumber,
God in mine ever-living soul, God in mine
serenity.

—COLLECTED BY ALEXANDER CARMICHAEL
IN THE NINETEENTH CENTURY AND USED IN
AVERY BROOKE'S CELTIC PRAYERS

Father, we come thirsty and hungry, not only for the food we are about to eat, but especially for Your presence in our lives. As we eat and drink, help us to remember that only Your love will quench our spiritual thirst and Your Spirit will satisfy our deepest longings. In Jesus' name. Amen.

Bless, O Father, Your gifts to our use and us to Your service; for Christ's sake. Amen.

Gracious God, we know that if we have food in the refrigerator, a roof over our heads, and a few clothes in the closet, we are better off than most other people in the world. May we be content with what we have. And help us to remember not to put our hope in things, but in You, the One who provides us with everything we need and enjoy, including this food. Amen.

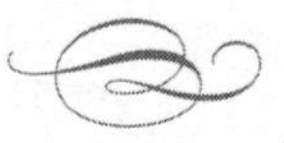

Loving God, as we sit down again at this table, we want to thank You today for creating us with the ability to taste so many good things. Not only have You provided ample food for us, but You gave us taste buds that relish the food placed before us. For this and for the many other blessings of this day, we thank You. Amen.

## For Everything Give Thanks

For all that God in mercy sends,
For health and children, home and friends,
For comfort in the time of need,
For every kindly word and deed,
For happy thoughts and holy talk,
For guidance in our daily walk,
For everything give thanks!

For beauty in this world of ours,
For verdant grass and lovely flowers,
For song of birds, for hum of bees,
For refreshing summer breeze,
For hill and plain, for streams and wood,
For the great ocean's mighty flood,
For everything give thanks!

For sweet sleep which comes with night,
For the returning morning light,
For the bright sun that shines on high,
For the stars glittering in the sky,
For these and everything we see,
O Lord, our hearts we lift to Thee
For everything give thanks!

—Helena Isabella Tupper

We ask You, Father, to be present at our table, to bless this food, and to make us truly thankful for all Your mercies. Amen.

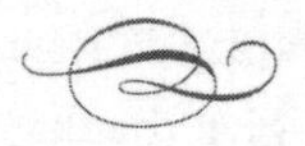

Giver of all, we are thankful for all that You have given us. Help us to remember daily that life is not about things or possessions, but about love. Let us show Your love in all we do and say, as You have shown love in providing this meal for us. Amen.

Father, how great is the love You have bestowed on us, that we should be called children of God. Bless this meal that it may strengthen us to do good things that will make You proud of us, Your children. Amen.

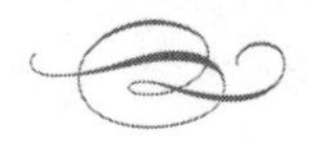

Dear Lord, as we bow our heads today to say grace, we are again reminded of the amazing grace You offered to us through Your Son, Jesus Christ, and throughout every day of our lives. Give us grateful hearts and grace-full hearts, as we accept the gift of the food so lovingly prepared for us. Teach us to extend grace to one another as You have so freely offered it to us. Amen.

Lord, we pray that You will be merciful to us and watch over us. Bless this food to our use and draw us closer to You. Through the name of our Lord and Savior Jesus Christ. Amen.

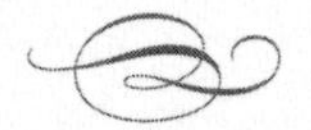

We accept, Lord, these gifts from You because You are the Giver of every good and perfect gift. While receiving Your blessings, teach us clearly that all we have—including our very lives—is because of Your generosity. In Christ's name we pray. Amen.

Lord, we need Your love and compassion. Come to us here, today, around our table, among all our friends and family. Fill us with Your love until we're bursting at the seams, until it hurts. Help us to look at others as You look at us, for we never know what another soul is feeling or going through. Lord, keep us from becoming cold and hardened by the world. Teach us your compassion; may we always be willing to help our neighbors without first having to be asked. Please bless our meal, and may it well nourish our bodies so that we may do Your good work. Amen.

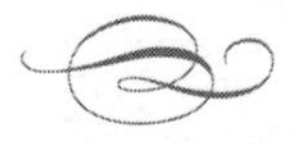

Dear Lord, we praise You for the love in our family and we ask Your blessings on us as we prepare to eat together. We thank You for this food and for the one who has prepared it. Be with us as we strive to serve You better. In Jesus' name we pray. Amen.

Help us remember, Lord, Your tender mercies and Your loving-kindnesses, which have always existed. Because of Your mercy, think of us, teach us, and make us thankful for these blessings, which are now spread before us. Amen.

Lord, send us anywhere, only accompany us.
Place any burden upon us, only sustain us.
Sever any tie, save that which binds us to thy heart.
Bless this food to the nourishment of our bodies
And our souls to the service of Christ.

—Robert E. Lee

Thank You for the wind and rain
and sun and pleasant weather,
Thank You for this our food
and that we are together.

—Mennonite blessing

Almighty God, we thank You for every good and perfect gift and above all for the gift of Your Son, Jesus Christ our Lord, who is the Bread to our souls, as this food is to our bodies. Amen.

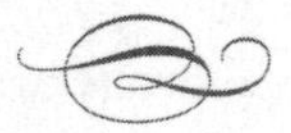

O Lord, as our bodies are sustained with this food, may our hearts be nourished with true friendship and our souls fed with truth. Amen.

Father, we are grateful that you have created us in Your own image. Thank You, Father, for the bodies that we have, and for the means that You give to supply them. Thank You for creative minds that discover many tasty ways to cook the food you give to us. Bless this food before us, and may it nourish our bodies well. Amen.

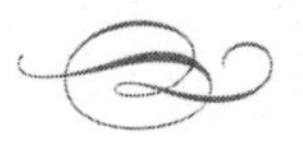

For this good fellowship, our Father, we thank You. We praise You for this nourishing food, Your loving care, and our family. Blend our hearts as we break bread together so that happiness may dwell in our home. Supply us with Your love, Lord, for the sake of Your Son, in whose name we pray. Amen.

Lord Jesus, You have told us not to worry, saying, "What shall we eat?" or "What shall we wear?" because our heavenly Father knows that we need all these things. Thank You for knowing what we need. Help us to remember this as we thank You for providing this food, which we are about to eat. And help us also to remember to seek first Your kingdom. Amen.

As You fed the hungry crowd by the Sea of Galilee, so also feed us, Lord. Refresh our bodies, and bring peace to our souls. We ask this in the name of Jesus, who is the Bread of Life. Amen.

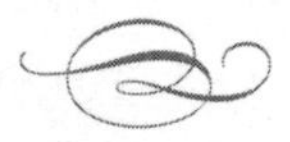

God,
You are the Maker of all things,
The Lover of all things,
The Provider of all things.
So thank You for making us, for loving us,
And for providing this meal
Which sits before us.
Amen.

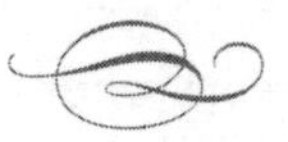

Great God, Giver of all good,
Accept our praise, and bless our food.
Grace, health, and strength to us afford,
Through Jesus Christ, our blessed Lord. Amen.

Lord, we thank You for the joys of life, for our daily bread, which nourishes our bodies, and for the night of sleep, which brings tranquillity and strength for the duties of a new day. Amen.

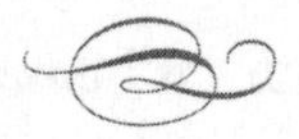

Be present at our table, Lord;
Be here and everywhere adored.
Thy creatures bless, and grant that we
May feast in paradise with Thee.

—JOHN WESLEY

We thank You, Lord, for our daily bread. May it strengthen and refresh our bodies. We pray that You will feed our souls with Your heavenly grace, through Jesus Christ, our Lord. Amen.

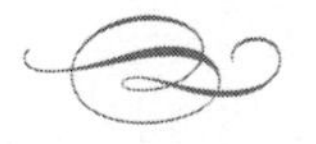

We must praise Thy goodness, that Thou hast left nothing undone to draw us to Thyself. But one thing we ask of Thee, our God, not to cease Thy work in our improvement. Let us tend towards Thee, no matter by what means, and be fruitful in good works, for the sake of Jesus Christ our Lord. Amen.

—LUDWIG VAN BEETHOVEN (1770–1827)

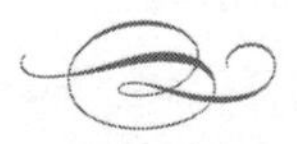

Give us grateful hearts, our Father, for all Thy mercies, and make us mindful of the needs of others; through Jesus Christ our Lord. Amen.

—THE BOOK OF COMMON PRAYER

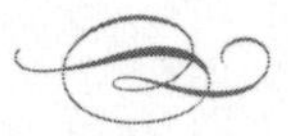

Lord, we want to stop and thank You for the joys and blessings we have every day—the love of this family, the fellowship of friends, our pets to lift our spirits, and now this food to eat. We also especially praise You for Your love, which was shown to us through the life and death and resurrection of Jesus Christ. Bless this food, and may we use it to continue living in service to You. Amen.

Lord God, heavenly Father, bless us and these Your gifts, which we receive from Your bountiful goodness; through Jesus Christ our Lord. Amen.

Lord, we begin this meal by giving thanks
to You.
This food is the gift of Your creation.
Protect that creation from all harm and hatred.
May we cherish the earth and all who partake
of its richness.
May we choose life and peace
so that we and all Your children may live.
We offer our thanks to You, our God of peace,
through Jesus, the Prince of Peace.
Amen.

—SCJ Office of Justice and Peace, Priests of the Sacred Heart, Hales Corners, Wisconsin

We thank You, O God our Father, for Your watchful care over us. Protect us from all evil and harm, and guard and guide us in all our ways. Bless this food to our use and us to Your service. In Jesus' name. Amen.

Gracious God, may the food we are about to eat strengthen our bodies, and may Your Holy Spirit strengthen and refresh our souls. Through Jesus Christ. Amen.

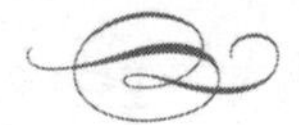

Dear God, You have called us to be the salt of the earth. May our words at this table be seasoned with grace. You have also called us to be the light of the world. May this food nourish us so that Your love will shine on us and all those we meet. In Jesus' name. Amen.

As we bow before You, heavenly Father, we realize that Your love has no limit, and we want to rest in this love throughout the remainder of the day. May the renewed strength obtained from this food be spent in Your service. Amen.

Holy God, we are grateful for all the blessings that You see fit to give us. Help us to use this food for Your good purpose. In Your name we pray. Amen.

Heavenly Father, make us thankful to You and mindful of others, as we receive these blessings. In Jesus' name. Amen.

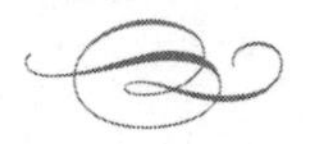

Help us, Lord, to seek first the kingdom of God and Your righteousness, and to know, therefore, that we shall never lack any good thing. We thank You again for all these blessings You have provided. Amen.

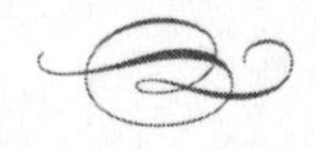

Father, we thank Thee for this food,
for health and strength and all things good.
May others all these blessings share,
and hearts be grateful everywhere.

—TRADITIONAL, CIRCA 1800S

God of life, no matter how much we think we support ourselves, it is You who sustains us. You created the earth, the plants, and the animals. All we have to do is care for your creation. Help us to use your gifts wisely. Amen.

We thank You, our Father, that You who clothe the lilies of the field and feed the birds of the air will also care for us. We know it is by Your graciousness that we are clothed and fed. Amen.

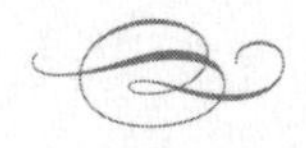

Holy God, Thank You for mealtime, let us use it as an opportunity to relax. Help us to use these moments for Your good, and to rest and refuel our bodies. We thank You for the meal set before us. Please bless it and the hands that so lovingly prepared it for us. Amen.

Heavenly Father, accept our thanks for this meal
And all our other blessings.
Bless those we love and are absent from us.
Give us each a strong will, a kind heart,
A firm faith, a quiet mind,
And grant us thy peace. Amen.

—Robin Johnson

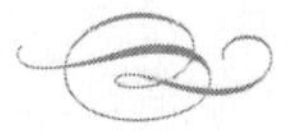

Blessed are You, O Lord God,
King of the universe,
for You give us food to sustain our lives
and make our hearts glad;
through Jesus Christ our Lord. Amen.

Father God,
Thank you for loving us. Thank you for your grace when we push you away. Thank You for Your mercy when we turn our backs on You. Help us to understand that no matter what we do, there is always a place for us at Your table. May we always welcome You at ours. Please bless this food before us. Amen.

O Lord God, heavenly Father, bless us and these Thy gifts, which we shall accept from Thy tender goodness. Give us food and drink. Also for our souls unto life eternal, and make us partakers of Thy heavenly table through Jesus Christ. Amen.

—AMISH PRAYER

We thank You for the good things, Lord,
that come from You above.
Please bless this food and help us learn
to live a life of love.
Amen.

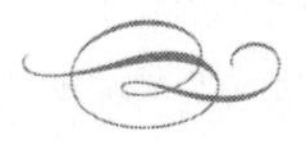

Make us remember, O God, that every day is Thy gift, and ought to be used according to Thy command; through Jesus Christ our Lord.

—SAMUEL JOHNSON (1709–1784)

Dear God,

To see a crimson sunset,

To hear the ticking of a clock or the purring of a cat,

To feel the splash of cold rain and the warmth of a hearth fire,

To smell the tangy sweetness of an orange, or the perfume of the one we love,

To taste so many flavors and enjoy this food before us,

For all these gifts we thank You.

Lord, teach us to appreciate these senses You have given to us,

For we know that there are those who are unable to enjoy these things.

It is for them that we now pray.

Amen.

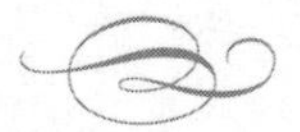

Let Thy blessing rest upon us of this family. In every condition secure our hearts to Thyself, and make us ever to approve ourselves sincere and faithful in Thy service.

—John Wesley (1703–1791)

O Lord of heaven, and earth, and sea,
To Thee all praise and glory be!
How shall we show our love to Thee,
Giver of all?
For peaceful homes, and healthful days,
For all the blessings earth displays,
We owe Thee thankfulness and praise,
Giver of all!

—Bishop Christopher Wordsworth (1807–1885)

Blessed are You,
O Lord our God,
Eternal King,
Who feeds the whole world
With Your goodness,
With grace, with loving-kindness,
And with tender mercy.

You give food to all flesh,
For Your loving-kindness endures forever.
Through Your great goodness,
Food has never failed us.
O may it not fail us forever,
For Your name's sake, since You
Nourish and sustain all living things
And do good to all,
And provide food for all Your creatures
Whom You have created.

Blessed are You, O Lord,
Who gives food to all.

—A HEBREW BERAKHAH (BLESSING)

Dear God,
Our bodies hunger for food,
But our souls hunger for You.
No food can fill our souls,
Only You can satisfy our deepest needs
Until we are full.
So thank You for this food we are about to eat,
And please keep us full,
body and soul.
Amen.

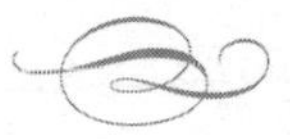

Dear God,

We worry so much about what will happen to us. Help us to know that just as You care for the lilies of the field and the birds in the air, so will You care for us. You have proved that by providing the meal before us. Thank You for loving us. Amen.

4

# Graces from the Bible

The eyes of all look expectantly to You,
And You give them their food in due season.
You open Your hand
And satisfy the desire of every living thing.
—PSALM 145:15–16

Blessed are You, LORD God of Israel, our
Father, forever and ever . . .
Both riches and honor come from You,
And You reign over all.
In Your hand is power and might;
In Your hand it is to make great
And to give strength to all.
Now therefore, our God,
We thank You
And praise Your glorious name.

—1 CHRONICLES 29:10, 12–13

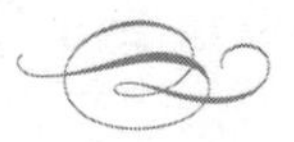

Make a joyful shout to the LORD, all you lands!
Serve the LORD with gladness;
Come before His presence with singing.
Know that the LORD, He is God;
It is He who has made us, and not we ourselves;
We are His people and the sheep of His pasture.
Enter into His gates with thanksgiving,
And into His courts with praise.
Be thankful to Him, and bless His name.
For the LORD is good;
His mercy is everlasting,
And His truth endures to all generations.

—PSALM 100

Bless the LORD, O my soul;
And all that is within me, bless His holy name!
Bless the LORD, O my soul,
And forget not all His benefits.

—PSALM 103:1–2

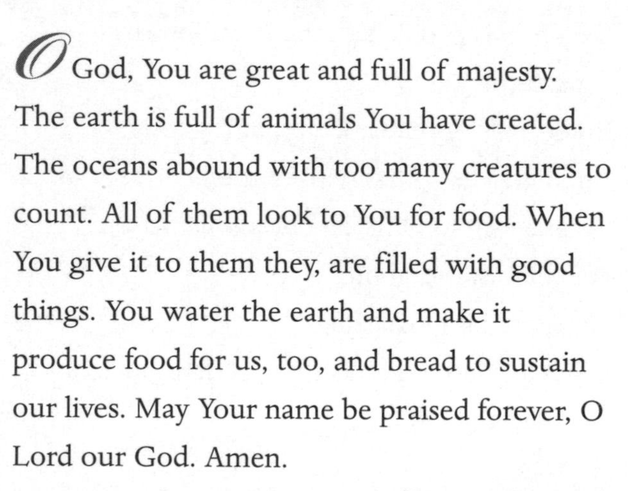

O God, You are great and full of majesty. The earth is full of animals You have created. The oceans abound with too many creatures to count. All of them look to You for food. When You give it to them they, are filled with good things. You water the earth and make it produce food for us, too, and bread to sustain our lives. May Your name be praised forever, O Lord our God. Amen.

—BASED ON PSALM 104

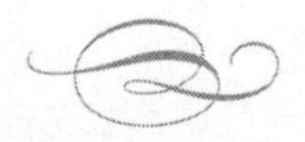

The eyes of all wait upon Thee
and Thou givest them their meat in due season.
Thou openest Thy hand
and fillest all things living with plenteousness.

We thank Thee, O Lord, for these Thy gifts
and beseech Thee to grant that whether we eat
or drink or whatsoever we do, all may be done to
Thy glory.

—ADAPTED FROM PSALM 104:27–28

Eat your bread with joy,
And drink your wine with a merry heart.

—ECCLESIASTES 9:7

When I consider your heavens, the work of your fingers,
the moon and stars, which you have set in place,
what is man that you are mindful of him?
. . . You made him ruler over the works of your hands. . . .
all flocks and herds, and the beasts of the field,
the birds of the air, and the fish of the sea,
all that swim the paths of the seas.
O LORD, our Lord, how majestic is your name
in all the earth!

—PSALM 8: 3, 4, 6-9 (NIV)

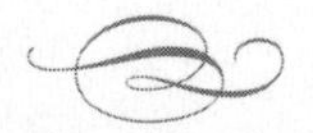

Give thanks to the LORD, for he is good; his love endures forever . . . He satisfies the thirsty and fills the hungry with good things. Amen.

—PSALM 107:1, 9 NIV

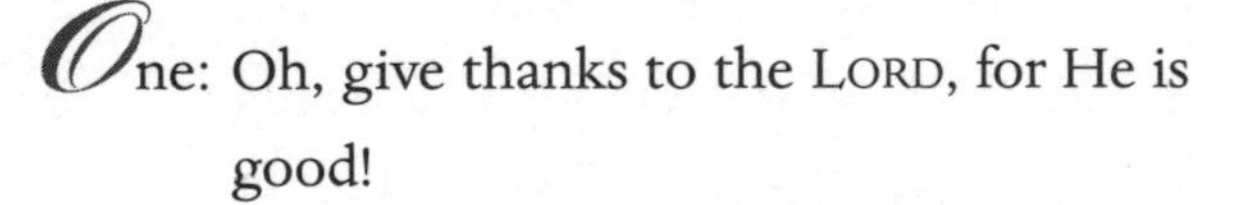

One: Oh, give thanks to the LORD, for He is good!

All: For His mercy endures forever . . .

One: Who remembered us in our lowly state,

All: For His mercy endures forever . . .

One: Who gives food to all flesh,

All: For His mercy endures forever . . .

One: Oh, give thanks to the God of heaven!

All: For His mercy endures forever.

—PSALM 136:1, 23, 25–26

Praise the LORD!
Praise the LORD, O my soul! . . .
Happy is he who has the God of Jacob for his help,
Whose hope is in the LORD his God . . .
Who executes justice for the oppressed,
Who gives food to the hungry.
The LORD gives freedom to the prisoners.

—PSALM 146:1, 5, 7

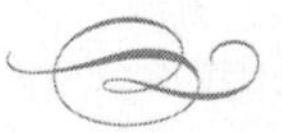

Sing to the LORD with thanksgiving;
Sing praises on the harp to our God,
Who covers the heavens with clouds,
Who prepares rain for the earth,
Who makes grass to grow on the mountains.
He gives to the beast its food,
And to the young ravens that cry.

—PSALM 147:7–9

The grace of the Lord Jesus Christ, and the love of God, and the communion of the Holy Spirit be with you all. Amen.

—2 CORINTHIANS 13:14

Ask, and it will be given to you; seek, and you will find; knock, and it will be opened to you. For everyone who asks receives, and he who seeks finds, and to him who knocks it will be opened.

—MATTHEW 7:7–8

# 5

# *Poetic Graces*

Lord, behold our family here assembled.
We thank you for this place in which we dwell,
for the love that unites us,
for the peace accorded us this day,
for hope with which we expect the morrow;
for the health, the work, the food and the bright skies
that make our lives delightful;
for our friends in all parts of the earth. Amen.

—Robert Louis Stevenson (1850–1894)

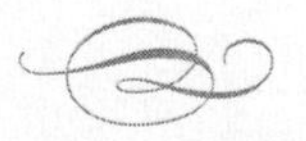

Praised be my Lord for our
Mother the Earth, which
Sustains us and keeps us and
Brings forth diverse fruits,
And flowers of many colors—
And grass.

—St. Francis of Assisi (1182–1226)
*The Canticle of the Creatures*

He prayest best, who loveth best
All things both great and small;
For the dear God who loveth us,
He made and loveth all.

—Samuel Taylor Coleridge (1772–1834)

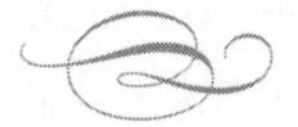

Lord, make me an instrument
of Your peace.
where there is hatred, let me sow love;
where there is injury, pardon;
where there is doubt, faith;
where there is darkness, light;
and where there is sadness, joy.

O Divine Master,
grant that I may not so much seek to be
consoled as to console;
to be understood as to understand;
to be loved as to love;
for it is in giving that we receive,
it is in pardoning that we are pardoned,
and it is in dying that we are born to
eternal life.
Amen.

—St. Francis of Assisi (1182–1226)

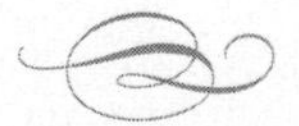

Great God, accept our gratitude,
For the great gifts on us bestowed—
For raiment, shelter, and for food.
Great God, our gratitude we bring,
Accept our humble offering,
For all the gifts on us bestowed,
Thy name be evermore adored.

—JOSEPHINE DELPHINE HENDERSON HEARD (1861–1921)

Day by day, dear Lord,
Of Thee three things I pray;
To see Thee more clearly,
Love Thee more dearly,
Follow Thee more nearly,
Day by day.

—RICHARD OF CHICHESTER (CIRCA 1197–1253)

O Lord, that lends me life,
Lend me a heart replete with thankfulness!

—WILLIAM SHAKESPEARE (1564–1616)

Thou has given so much to me,
Give one thing more, a grateful heart,
Not thankful when it pleaseth me,
As if Thy blessings had spare days;
But such a heart, whose pulse may be
Thy praise.

—GEORGE HERBERT (1593–1633)

Let us with a gladsome mind
Praise the Lord for He is kind;
For His mercies aye endure,
Ever faithful, ever sure.

All things living He doth feed,
His full hand supplies their need:
For His mercies aye endure,
Ever faithful, ever sure.

—JOHN MILTON (1608–1674)

The Lord my pasture shall prepare,
And feed me with a shepherd's care.
His presence shall my wants supply,
And guard me with a watchful eye.

—JOSEPH ADDISON (1672–1719)

O Thou, who kindly dost provide
For every creature's want!
We bless Thee, God of nature wide,
For all Thy goodness lent;
And, if it please Thee, heavenly Guide,
May never worse be sent;
But, whether granted or denied,
Lord, bless us with content!

—ROBERT BURNS (1759–1796)

I thank You God for most this amazing
day:for the leaping greenly spirits of trees
and a blue true dream of sky; and for
everything
which is natural which is infinite which is yes

—E. E. CUMMINGS

Without Thy sunshine and Thy rain;
We would not have the golden grain;
Without Thy love we'd not be fed;
We thank Thee for our daily bread.

—ANONYMOUS

Dear God,

Thank you for the gifts of sight, hearing, and speech.<br>
Help us not to take them for granted<br>
And to use all the gifts you give us to help others.<br>
And help us also to remember,<br>
That when bodies are not so agile<br>
Or minds are not so quick,<br>
That each of us nevertheless has special gifts<br>
To share with one another.<br>
We give you thanks for the gift of this food<br>
And for all the talents and abilities we have received<br>
Through your generous love.<br>
Amen.

—Helen Keller

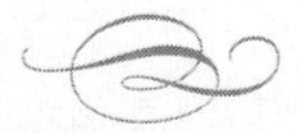

6

# Graces from Other Cultures

God, bless to us our bread,
And give bread to all those who are hungry,
And hunger for justice to all those who are fed,
God, bless to us our bread.

—ARGENTINEAN PRAYER

As plentiful as the grass that grows,
Or the sand on the shore,
Or the dew on the lea,
So the blessings of the King of Grace
On every soul that was, that is, or will be.

—TRADITIONAL IRISH BLESSING

## A GAELIC BLESSING

May the road rise to meet you,
may the wind be always at your back,
may the sun shine warm on your face,
the rain fall softly on your fields;
and until we meet again,
may God hold you in the palm of His hand.

—AUTHOR UNKNOWN

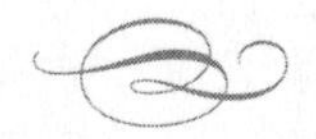

## A Parting Blessing

The Lord bless us and keep us.
The Lord make His face to shine upon us
and be gracious unto us,
The Lord lift up the light of His countenance
upon us and give us peace.

—Based on Psalm 67:1

## English Prayer

Give me a good digestion, Lord,
and also something to digest;
Give me a healthy body, Lord,
and sense to keep it at its best;

Give me a healthy mind, good Lord,
to keep the good and pure in sight,
Which, seeing sin, is not appalled,
But finds a way to set it right.

Give me a mind that is not bound,
that does not whimper, whine, or sigh.
Don't let me worry overmuch
about the fussy thing called I.

Give me a sense of humor, Lord;
Give me the grace to see a joke,
To get some happiness from life
and pass it on to other folk.

—This ancient prayer, found on the wall of Chester Cathedral in England, has been attributed to Thomas H. B. Webb.

## An Irish Blessing

May there always be work for your hands
to do
May your purse always hold a coin or two
May the sun always shine upon your
windowpane
May a rainbow be certain to follow each rain
May the hand of a friend always be near to
you and
May God fill your heart with gladness to
cheer you.

—Author unknown

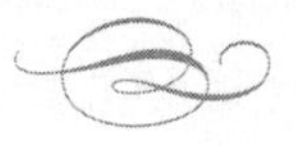

## Prayer from the Netherlands

O God who makes a thousand flowers to blow,
Who makes both grains and fruits to grow,
Hear our prayer;
Bless this food
And bring us peace.
Amen.

—Author unknown

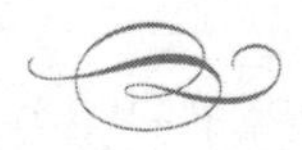

## African Grace

The bread is pure and fresh,
the water is cool and clear.
Lord of all life, be with us.
Lord of all, be near.

Thank You very, very much,
My God, thank You.
Give me food today,
For my sustenance every day.
Thank You very, very much.
—TRADITIONAL SAMBURU BLESSING, KENYA

May the abundance of this table
Never fail and never be less,
Thanks to the blessings of God,
Who has satisfied our needs.
To Him be the glory forever.
Amen.

—ARMENIAN GRACE, LEBANON

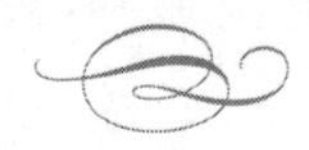

Though our mouths were full of song as
the sea,
And our tongues of exultation as the multitude
of its waves,
And our lips of praise as the wide-extended
firmament;
Though our eyes shone with light like the sun
and the moon,
And our hands were spread forth like the eagles
of heaven,
And our feet were swift as hinds, we should
still be unable
To thank Thee and bless Thy name,
Oh Lord our God and God of our fathers, for
one thousandth
or one ten-thousandth of the bounties which
Thou hast bestowed
Upon our fathers and upon us.

—The Hebrew Prayer Book

Aloha to God above.
*Aloha*, a word that means
I love you.
*Mahalo*, too, means
I thank you.
Mahalo, aloha to God.
(Ma/ha/low)

—HAWAIIAN GRACE

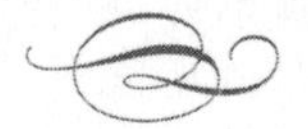

No ordinary meal—a sacrament awaits us.
On our tables daily spread,
For men are risking lives on sea and land,
That we may dwell in safety and be fed.

—Scottish grace

Been out on the range,
All dusty and tired.
Been ridin' and ropin' all day,
Around the chuck wagon.

We bow down our heads,
And sing out the cowboys' grace.
Allelujah, Amen, Amen.
Allelujah, Amen, Amen.

—A Cowboy grace

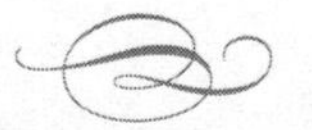

# 7

# *Musical Graces*

Praise God, from whom all blessings flow
Praise Him, all creatures here below;
Praise Him above, ye heavenly hosts
Praise Father, Son, and Holy Ghost.

—Bishop Thomas Ken (1637–1711)
Doxology

## Father, We Thank Thee for the Night

Father, we thank Thee for the night,
And for the pleasant morning light;
For rest and food and loving care,
And all that makes the world so fair.
Help us to do the things we should,
To be to others kind and good;
In all we do, in work or play,
To love Thee better day by day.

—Rebecca J. Weston, 1885

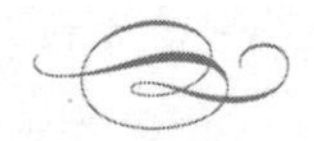

## Give Thanks

Give thanks with a grateful heart,
  give thanks to the Holy One,
give thanks because He's given
  Jesus Christ his Son.
And now let the weak say, "I am strong";
  let the poor say, "I am rich"
Because of what the Lord has done for us.
  Give thanks!

—Henry Smith, 1978

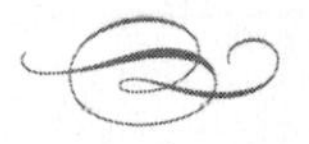

Bless this day, bless those here,
Come, O Lord, share this hour;
May our lives glow with peace,
Blest with love and Your power.
Friendship and love may they bloom and grow,
Bloom and grow forever.
Bless our friends, bless this food,
Bless all mankind forever.

—To be sung to the tune of Edelweis

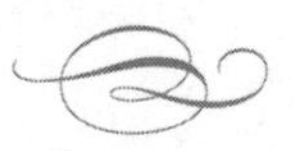

## BE KNOWN TO US IN BREAKING BREAD

Be known to us in breaking bread,
But do not then depart;
Savior, abide with us, and spread
Thy table in our heart.

There eat with us in love divine;
Thy body and Thy blood,
That living bread, that heavenly wine,
Be our immortal food.

—JAMES MONTGOMERY, 1825

## Fairest Lord Jesus

Fairest Lord Jesus,
Ruler of all nature,
O Thou of God and man the Son;
Thee will I cherish, Thee will I honour,
Thou, my soul's glory, joy, and crown.

Fair are the meadows,
Fairer still the woodlands,
Robed in the blooming garb of spring;
Jesus is fairer, Jesus is purer,
Who makes the woeful heart to sing.

Fair is the sunshine,
Fairer still the moonlight,
And all the twinkling, starry host;
Jesus shines brighter, Jesus shines purer,
Than all the angels heaven can boast.

—Munster Gesangbuch, 1677

## All Things Bright and Beautiful

All things bright and beautiful,
All creatures, great and small,
All things wise and wonderful,
The Lord God made them all.

Each little flower that opens,
Each little bird that sings,
He made their glowing colors,
He made their tiny wings.

The tall trees in the greenwood,
The meadows where we play,
The rushes by the water
We gather every day—

He gave us eyes to see them,
And lips that we might tell
How great is God Almighty,
Who has made all things well.

—Cecil Francis Alexander, 1848

## Come, Ye Thankful People, Come

Come, ye thankful people, come
Raise the song of harvest home;
All is safely gathered in,
Ere the winter storms begin;
God, our Maker, doth provide
For our wants to be supplied;
Come to God's own temple, come,
Raise the song of harvest home.

—Henry Alford (1810–1871)

# 8

# Graces for Holidays and Holy Days

O holy child of Bethlehem, this waiting season of Advent is coming to an end. As we anticipate opening our gifts and sharing this wonderful meal, we are making room for You, our special Guest. Come join us and bless us with the gift of Your presence. Amen.

## New Year's Eve

God, as we approach the end of another year, we thank You for all that we have experienced these twelve months. You have been with us, as You have promised, through the good and the bad times. We thank You for providing for us in every way and trust that You will guide us through this coming year. Bless this food and bless us all as we anticipate another year of serving You. In Christ's name. Amen.

We pause to give thanks for Your goodness to us, Father. You have brought us on our way to the end of another year. You have blessed us with food and surrounded us with Your constant love. Receive our humble thanks in the Master's name. Amen.

## New Year's Day

As we gather around this table today to greet the New Year, we are thankful, Lord, that You have blessed us so richly in the past year. We pray that You will watch over us and guide our paths today and all year long. We ask in Jesus' name. Amen.

Another year has dawned upon us. We greet this day with gratitude and thanksgiving in our hearts. Inspire us to be useful and effective throughout the coming days. We bless Your name. Amen.

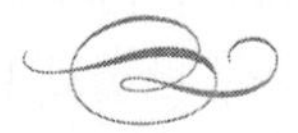

## New Year's Poem

Another year is dawning!
Dear Father, let it be
In working or in waiting
Another year with Thee!
Another year of leaning
Upon Thy loving breast,
Another year of trusting,
Of quiet, happy rest.

Another year of service,
Of witness for Thy love;
Another year of training
For holier work above.
Another year is dawning!
Dear Father, let it be
On earth, or else in heaven,
Another year for Thee.

—Frances R. Havergal (1836–1879)

As we commence a brand new year,
May we learn from the mistakes we have made.

We resolve this year to walk with You
From beginning to end, through good and bad.

Make each day an opportunity
To show Your love to those around us.

—ANONYMOUS

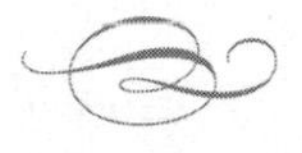

## Ash Wednesday

You, Lord, are our strength. We need Your forgiveness. On this day of penitence, draw near and help us to be thankful for Your sacrificial love. We are grateful for this meal and for Your boundless grace. Through Jesus Christ our Lord. Amen.

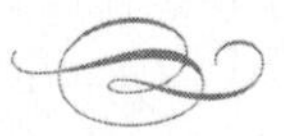

## Maundy Thursday (Thursday of Holy Week)

Our Father, as we recall the meaning of the Last Supper of our Lord with His disciples, our hearts are warmed by His humbleness. Bless us with that spirit as we partake of this meal. We praise You for His example and His redemptive work. In His name we pray. Amen.

## Good Friday

Our Father, we bow with heavy hearts when we think of the sacrificial love of our blessed Savior. We think now of Golgotha and the cross He bore for us. Help us to live in His forgiving presence. We thank You now for Your unending love. In the Master's name. Amen.

## Easter

Dear Lord, on this day of special celebration for the resurrection of our Lord, we praise You for His victory over death. Thank You for the promise of eternal life that we have in You. Thank You for Your Son and His life here on earth. We are humbled because He was willing to die on the cross for our sins. Help us always to be mindful of that sacrificial love. Be with us as we strive to live to be worthy of the final resurrection, which we will have with You. For we pray in the blessed Savior's name. Amen.

Joyfully, this Easter day,
I kneel, a little child, to pray,
Jesus, who hath conquered death,
Teach me, with my every breath,
To praise and worship Thee.

—SHARON BANIGAN

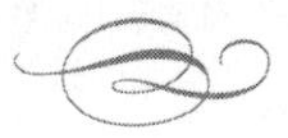

The day is coming to a close,
And, like the disciples on the road to Emmaus,
We pause to break bread together.
May our eyes be opened, and in this act of common sharing,
may we see the risen Lord in one another.
May we see the Lord of Life in our food, our conversation,
and lives shared in common.
May the blessing of God, His peace and love,
rest upon our table.
Alleluia! Amen.

—EVENING MEAL BLESSING FOR EASTER

Father God, the new life of spring is so exciting! Thank You for the bright colors of the flowers, the carpet of new green grass, and the warmer days which beckon us outside. The beauty of Your world is astonishing, Lord, and we thank You for allowing us to be part of it. Please bless the meal before us. Amen.

God of life,
As the days grow warmer, the signs of spring surround us. We remember that each year You make the earth new again, just as You make us new through Jesus Christ. Thank You for springtime, and for the feeling of a fresh start. Thank you for giving us this food. Amen.

God, our Creator, when we look around us and see the world You have created, we are awed and amazed. Only You could have the power and talent to make such a world. Thank You for eyes to see such beauty. Thank You for ears to hear the music of birds singing, crickets chirping, and water rippling. And now, we thank You for the food that is so essential for our lives and keeps us able to enjoy all the wonders of Your creation. Amen.

## Memorial Day

O God, we thank You that You have preserved for us a nation with liberty and justice. Help us this day to honor the men and women who fought and died for our country. We thank You for the spirit of patriotism that binds us together. Grant that all our nation may serve You first and foremost. Amen.

God of peace,
We recall today the words of Jesus,
"Blessed are the peacemakers;
they shall be called the sons and daughters of God."
As we remember all who have died because of war,
inspire the leaders of all nations
to turn away from war and work for peace.
Help us also to live in peace with one another,
and with peoples of every nation, race, and creed.
Bless this food we share
as we celebrate this day with our family and friends.
Amen.

## Vacation

God, we thank You for this special time of the year when we can relax and get away from some of the stresses of work. Thank You that we have the privilege of leisure time, which many people in the world do not have. We ask Your blessing on our fun and on this food. Amen.

God of joy,
The wonders of Your earth never cease to amaze us: the crickets chirping, the warmth of the sun. Thank You for summer, which brings us such joy in exploring, and a time of growth for the plants, which turn into the food before us. Bless this meal we pray. Amen.

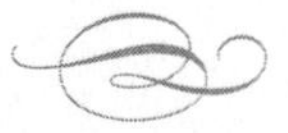

## Pentecost

Almighty and most merciful God, grant, we beseech Thee, that by the indwelling of Thy Holy Spirit, we may be enlightened and strengthened for Thy service; through Jesus Christ our Lord. Amen.

—The Book of Common Prayer

## Independence Day

O God our Creator,
we thank You for our country,
for the freedom and opportunity it gives us,
and for its beauty and bounty.
As we celebrate with this meal,
we ask You to bless our food and to
bless our nation.
Help us to choose leaders inspired by its ideals
and mindful of the rights of all people.
Help us to use our nation's gifts wisely,
and to extend Your care to the
needy of the world.
We ask this through Christ our Lord.
Amen.

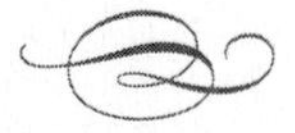

God of Love,
We are reminded today, on Independence Day, of all the freedoms that we enjoy and take for granted. We are so thankful to be living here, where we have, among others, the freedom to love You openly. Father, we're grateful our founding fathers had a vision of a greater life. Please guide our country's leaders today as they strive to continue spreading that vision of a greater life. Please help us to remember that it is more than a freedom, but a responsibility to spread Your love to all the world. Bless us now as we celebrate the day. Amen.

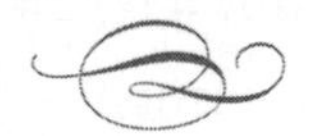

## Prayer for the Nation

Almighty God, in whose righteous will all things are and were created; You have gathered our people into a great nation and have given them the treasures of the land and of the sea. Make us reverent in the use of freedom, just in the exercise of power, and generous in the protection of the weak. Bless the president of our nation and all in authority. To our legislators and local representatives give insight and faithfulness, that our laws may clearly speak the right and our judges purely interpret it. May wisdom and knowledge be the stability of our times and our deepest trust be in You, the Lord of nations and the only righteous Sovereign of all people. Amen.

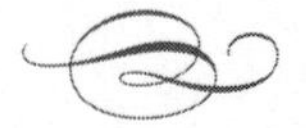

## Labor Day

Lord, we know that You are the Source of all of our blessings. We thank You for this food and for all the men and women whose hard work has made it possible for us to have it so conveniently. We are grateful for the opportunity to work and to provide for ourselves and those we love. We thank You now for the abundance of blessings You have bestowed on us. Please be with those who are less fortunate than we are, and help us to share the fruits of our labor with them. For we pray through Christ. Amen.

Dear God, we realize that every day people work hard to provide our needs from the abundance of Your creation. Thank You today for those who have labored to make our lives easier, and especially for those who labored to provide us with this food. Amen.

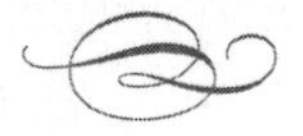

## First Days of Fall

Almighty God, as the days grow shorter and the air grows colder, we realize that winter is near. Thank You for being with us through the heat of the summer and for protecting us in the cold of winter. We are grateful to You for providing our needs all year and through all the seasons. Bless this food that warms and fills us. Amen.

## Veterans Day

Father, we thank You for the men and women who have been willing to risk many things to serve their country—many risking death. We are grateful for their service in order to protect the freedom of our country. Father, teach us to think less of ourselves, and more of You, for it was Your one and only son who paid the ultimate sacrifice for our eternal freedom. Bless this meal as we honor our veterans. Amen.

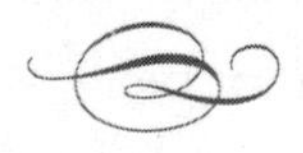

## THANKSGIVING

Bountiful God,
You have blessed us in many ways,
in the beauty and richness of our land,
and in the freedom we enjoy.
You have given us even greater gifts
in our family who loves and cares for us
and in the grace that allows us to know and
believe in You.
May we be grateful for all our blessings,
not just today, but every day.
Help us to turn our gratitude into action
by caring for those in need
and by working for a more just society.
Bless this wonderful meal before us and each of
us at this table.
Be with all those we love who are not here.
We give You thanks through Jesus our Lord.
Amen.

Dear Lord, today we are mindful of the countless blessings You have given us. We are grateful for our country in which we have the freedom to worship You as we see fit. Lord, we praise You for Your handiwork, for the beauty of nature, and for the enjoyment that it brings us. As we come together to eat this food, help us to make this and every day a day of thanksgiving to You. We pray this through Your Son. Amen.

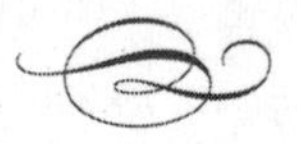

Lord, on this day of thanksgiving, we come to You to praise You for all that You have so generously given us. We know that all we have comes from You. We pray that You will help us to not be envious of what others have, but to be humbly grateful for the blessings we possess. Be with us now in our feast of thanksgiving, and keep us always humble in Your sight. In Jesus' name we pray. Amen.

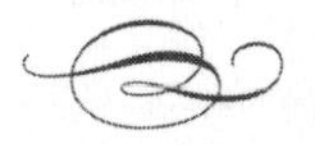

Gracious God,
It is obvious to see how much You care for us by looking at the bountiful spread on our table. Give us the love for others to share what You have given. Give us courage to show the love of Jesus with those who need Him, but don't know Him. Please bless this food before us. Amen.

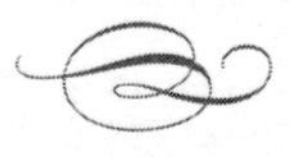

## Advent

Almighty God, we thank You for the promise of a Savior so long ago. Prepare our hearts to accept Him anew in the spirit of love and peace He brought into the world. Give us a true understanding of the meaning of Christmas and renew our spirits as we enter this holy season. Through Jesus Christ, our Lord. Amen.

## Christmas Eve

Holy God,

We praise Your name tonight as we celebrate the birth of the baby Jesus. We thank You for sending Him to us to teach us how to love and how to live. Help us to show that love in all our words and actions tonight and all year long. As we give and receive gifts tonight, may we remember that they are not the true celebration, but that Christ is the reason we are gathered together. Please bless this meal we are about to receive, and bless those who have lovingly prepared it. Open our hearts that we may invite Jesus in. Amen.

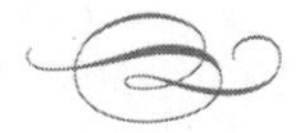

O holy Child of Bethlehem, this waiting season of Advent is coming to an end. As we anticipate opening our gifts and sharing this wonderful meal, we are making room for You, our special Guest. Come join us and bless us with the gift of Your presence. Amen.

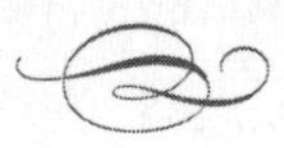

## Christmas Season

Great God,

You truly are the giver of all good things. Father, we thank You for all our blessings today: for our family and friends who love us, for warm beds and clothes to wear, and for plenty of food to eat. Most of all, Lord, we thank You for the greatest gift of all, Jesus, whose birth we celebrate today! May we always strive to be like Him and to spread His love to all the world. Please bless this meal, and bless us as we celebrate the day with love and laughter. Guide our paths today and always. In Jesus' holy name we pray. Amen.

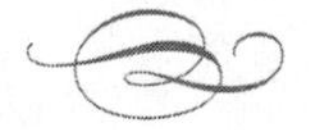

Lord, we thank You that You sent Your only Son to this world to reveal Your love for us. As we celebrate the day of His birth, we ask that You will be with all of Your children everywhere and bless them. Thank You for all the gifts You have bestowed upon us. Keep us humble and guide us as we try to be more like Christ. We praise You for Your unending love. It is through Your blessed Son that we pray. Amen.

What can I give Him
Poor as I am?
If I were a shepherd
I would bring a lamb,
If I were a wise man
I would do my part;
Yet what can I give Him—
Give Him my heart.

—CHRISTINA ROSSETTI

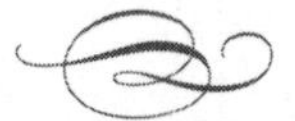

How silently, how silently,
The wondrous gift is given;
So God imparts to human hearts
The blessing of His heaven.

—PHILLIPS BROOKS

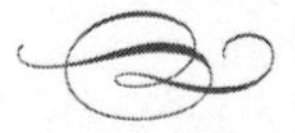

# 9
# Graces for Special Occasions

Lord, we have never gathered at this table and been so exhausted yet so joyful all at the same time. Our new baby has brought us so much happiness already, even as we're adjusting to life as an expanding family. When we look at our child, Father, we marvel that You could create something so perfect. Please guide us through these next months as we learn the true sacrifices parents make for their children. And Lord, please help us get through this meal without falling asleep. Amen.

—Anonymous

## New Baby

Lord, we praise You for the gift of life. We offer You humble thanks for this precious child whom You have entrusted to our care. We know that the family is the most important earthly institution that You have established, and we pray that You will guide us in making our home the place of love and understanding that You would have it to be. Please bless __________ with health and strength, and help us to provide the proper spiritual training. We want __________ to be like Jesus and to grow in wisdom and stature, and in favor with God and man. For we pray through His name. Amen.

## BIRTHDAY

Lord, today we come to thank You for bringing ____________ into the world and especially into our lives. It has been a joy to have another opportunity to show our love for ____________ and to celebrate in this special way. We ask Your blessings on our fun and laughter today, and on this food. In Jesus' name. Amen.

Father, we praise You that as the years pass, each one brings new blessings and joys. You have been generous with us throughout all our lives, and we are truly grateful. Now we thank You for the joy of birthday celebrations, for the blessings of the year that has passed, and for the hope and anticipation of the year to come. May each birthday find us closer to You. We pray in the Savior's name. Amen.

Lord, we invite You to join us at this birthday celebration for ______________, our special loved one. As we laugh and joke about the years that seem to have flown by, we want to take a moment to thank You for bringing this dear one into the world and for bringing him/her into our lives. We ask Your blessings on him/her for this next year. May it be filled with joy, fulfillment, peace, and love. In Jesus' name we pray. Amen.

## WEDDING

Lord, we thank You for the holiness of marriage and all that it represents. We come before You now to ask Your special blessing on the two people who will be married today. Grant that they will remain firm in their total commitment to each other and to You. Give them patience and understanding and help them to put You above all things. Please bless their new home and make it a place of peace and happiness. We thank You for Your continuing care for all Your children. We pray through Jesus. Amen.

## Anniversary

Dear Lord, we thank You that You have given us these precious years of life together. We are grateful that You have brought us through the trials as well as the joys of marriage and have given us so many of Your wonderful blessings. Help us always to remember the importance of our commitment to each other and to You. Help us to be patient, kind, and considerate with each other. Please continue to guide us in our efforts to make our home a place of love and peace. Be with us now and on our special day and throughout our lives. In Jesus' blessed name we pray. Amen.

God of love, we come with joy as we celebrate with ________________ and ______________ another year of marriage. We thank You for the love that has grown between them through the years and ask that You continue to bless their life together. May their love increase with each passing year—both for each other and for You. We ask Your blessings, now, on this food and our time of celebration. Amen.

## Mother's Day

Loving and nurturing God, we thank You today for our mother. We thank You that You instilled in her those tender, loving qualities that come only from You. Thank You for her many sacrifices for us, her patience, her strength, and hard work—even when no one has noticed. And now, we thank You for this food and for this time to celebrate Mom's special day. Amen.

## FATHER'S DAY

Heavenly Father, we thank You for our earthly father. Thank You for the wisdom and leadership he provides for us. We are grateful for his hard work and determination, which bring us so many opportunities. We thank You—and him—for all he has done through the years to help each one of us. We pray that he will continue to rely on Your strength as we grow together each day as a family. We thank You for this food and especially for Dad. Amen.

## Baptism

Our Father, we thank You for this joyful occasion, when our dear _____________ has become a member of Your kingdom. On this day of baptism we rejoice with the angels in heaven as we celebrate this special time in her/his life. We praise You for Your promise of salvation and Your willingness to let Your Son die on the cross for our sins. Thank You for Your grace and Your love, which we don't deserve, but will never let us go. In Jesus' name. Amen.

## Visitors in the Home

We thank You, our heavenly Father, for these guests who are gathered around this table. Strengthen the bond of our friendship as we partake of this provision for our bodies. Amen.

We thank You for the joy of friends and for the fellowship that graces this house. Give us grateful hearts for all Your tender care over us. Amen.

## Family Reunion

We praise You for bringing us together again as a family, and we ask Your blessing on this time we share. We thank You for the love and kinship that bind us together. We know that wherever we may be, we are a part of Your family. Now as we eat this meal together, we acknowledge all Your gifts to us and pray that we will remember You as the Giver of every good and perfect gift in the days ahead. Be with us now and in the days ahead when we are apart. In Christ's name we pray. Amen.

## First Day of School

Lord, we thank You for the opportunity to receive an education. As we start the year, help us to be receptive to new ideas and willing to work to accomplish worthwhile goals. Please be with our teachers and give them wisdom and patience in their dealings with us. In all that we study and do, Lord, help us to glorify You. In the Savior's name we pray. Amen.

## Family Member Absent

Gracious Lord, as we come before You with thanks for all Your gifts, which You have so generously given us, we ask Your blessing on our loved one ____________, who is absent from us. Please grant safety, health, and the sure sense of Your presence in all that he/she undertakes today. Be with all of us until we can be together again. Thank You for Your continued guidance and love. In Jesus' name we pray. Amen.

## Travel

Dear Lord, we know that You are present everywhere. We know that wherever we may go, You will be there also. We ask You now to be with us as we travel. Please protect us from danger and guide us to our destination. Help us to trust You to watch over us wherever we are, and please bring us safely home again. In Christ's name we pray. Amen.

## New Home

Lord, we come to You now asking that You bless us in our new home. We pray that You will help us to work together to make it a place of love, warmth, and happiness. Surround us with Your tender care and protect us from harm. We pray that all will be able to see the evidences of Your love in our home. Be with us in our efforts to glorify You. In Christ's name we pray. Amen.

## Picnic

Lord, as we are surrounded by Your handiwork, we praise You for its beauty. We thank You for the glory of nature and of this day. We see Your evidences in all that is around us, and we are mindful of Your amazing love for us. We are thankful for the changing of the seasons and the joy that each one brings to our lives. Be with us now as we eat this food, and accept our praise and thanks for Your generosity toward us. In the Savior's name we pray. Amen.

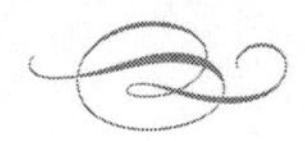

## Sabbath

Our Father, we thank You for this Sabbath day, which You have given us. Be with us now as we prepare our hearts and minds to worship You. We ask Your forgiveness for our failures this past week, and we ask Your guidance for the coming week as we try to live more like Christ. Help us always to be mindful of Your love for us. In the Savior's name. Amen.

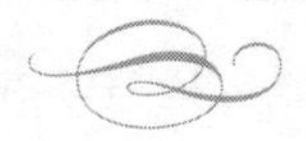

## Death of a Loved One

O God, we are once again reminded of the brevity of life. We are sad at the passing of this loved one, but help us to remember that there is a world far greater than this that comes after death. Please be with ___________ and ___________ and all of us in our grief, and help us to take comfort in the knowledge that our dear ______________ is in Your loving presence. We pray in the name of the One who died so that we all may have eternal life. Amen.

# 10

# *Evening Graces*

Our Father, bless our evening meal. Forgive all that You have seen wrong in us today, in thought or word or deed. And keep us this night in Your holy care. Through Jesus. Amen.

Lord, we thank You for Your love and Your gift of salvation. We ask Your forgiveness for all that we have done wrong today. Please help us as we try to be more like You. Thank You for the food we have before us now. May we be strengthened by it in order to serve You better. For we pray through Christ. Amen.

Lord Jesus, be our guest;
Our morning joy, our evening rest.
And with our daily bread, and part,
Bring peace and joy to every heart.
Amen.

—TRADITIONAL AMERICAN GRACE

As we lift up our hearts in thanksgiving for the blessings of the day that has passed, we pray that You will watch over us this night, and bring us to yet another day to work for You. We praise You for Your generosity toward us, and we pray that You will accept our thanks for this food. In Jesus' name. Amen.

We praise You, Lord, for the mercies of yet another day. We pray that You will accept our evening prayer of thanks for these provisions of Your love. Be with us tonight and bring us into a new day tomorrow. In Jesus' name. Amen.

Dear God,

As we sit here tonight, surrounded by the ones we love, let us forget all the things that went wrong today, and be thankful for all that went right. Amen.

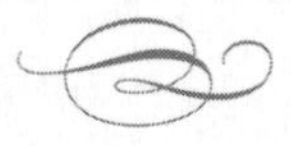

Lord, we thank You for the blessings we have already received this day—for honest work, for school and teachers, for good health, and for bringing us back home in safety. We thank You for this food and ask that You bless our conversation as we enjoy our evening meal. May the words of our mouths and the meditations of our hearts be acceptable in Your sight, O God, our strength and Redeemer. Amen.

# Our Family's Own Special Graces

# OUR FAMILY'S OWN SPECIAL GRACES

# Acknowledgments

Grateful acknowledgment is made to the following publishers for use of material from their previously published works. Every effort has been made to locate the original sources of these prayers. However, in many cases the sources may no longer be available or are attributed to many different sources. Inadvertent omissions, if called to the publisher's attention, will be noted in future editions.

Concordia Publishing House. *The Children's Hymnal.* 1955. Used by permission of Concordia Publishing House.

Cotner, June. *Graces.* New York: Harper Collins, 1994. Used by permission.

———. *Family Celebrations.* Kansas City, MO: Andrews McMeel, 1999. Used by permission.

The lines from "i thank You God for most this amazing". Copyright 1950, © 1978, 1991 by the Trustees for the E. E. Cummings Trust. Copyright © 1979 by George James Firmage, from COMPLETE POEMS: 1904-1962 by E. E. Cummings, edited by George J. Firmage. Used by permission of Liveright Publishing Corporation.

Hamma, Robert M. *Let's Say Grace.* Notre Dame, IN: Ave Maria Press, Inc., 1995. Used by permission.

Hays, Edward M. *Prayers for the Domestic Church*. Notre Dame, IN: Ave Maria Press, Inc., 1979. Used by permission.
Kelly, Marcia, and Jack Kelly. *100 Graces.* New York: Bell Tower, Harmony Books, Crown Publishers, 1992. Used by permission.
McElwain, Sarah, ed. *Saying Grace.* San Francisco: Chronicle Books, 2003. Used by permission.
Sandlin, John Lewis. *A Book of Table Graces.* Old Tappan, NJ: Fleming H. Revell, 1963. Used by permission of Fleming H. Revell.
Smith, Henry. "Give Thanks." Mobile, AL: Integrity's Hosanna! Music ASCAP, 1978. Used by permission.
The Upper Room. *Table Graces.* Nashville, TN: The Upper Room, 1953. Reprinted by permission of The Upper Room.
Tirabassi, Maren C., and Kathy Wonson Eddy. *Gifts of Many Cultures.* Cleveland, OH: Pilgrim Press, United Church Press, 1995. Used by permission.
Vineyard Books. *Youth Talks with God.* Adapted from prayers by Avery Brooke. Norton, CT: Vineyard Books.
Permission granted by Vineyard Books, Inc., P.O. Box 3315, Norton, CT 06820.